GUIDE TO MAXIMIZING RETIREMENT

GUIDE TO

MAXIMIZING RETIREMENT

6 KEY BUILDING BLOCKS TO SUCCESS

JOEL M. JOHNSON, CFP®

Printed in the United States of America.

ISBN: 978-1-63385-425-3

Designed and published by

Word Association Publishers
205 Fifth Avenue
Tarentum, Pennsylvania 15084

www.wordassociation.com
1.800.827.7903

CONTENTS

INTRODUCTION

What does retirement mean to you?

For some people, it is intimidating to think about retirement. When they go into retirement, there is a loss of purpose. There's a feeling of unease because they've been so busy for so long. Yet others feel a sense of relief. There's almost a sense of reward – because you've worked really hard and you've earned and deserve this. In some instances, one partner is very comfortable with the concept of retirement, however the other partner is not.

And so, retirement means different things to different people.

In this book, I will lay out the problems in planning for and having a successful retirement. I'll also share strategies to help you make sure that you are well-positioned to have the best probability of maximizing the quality of life in your retirement.

Let's think about the challenges that face the average retiree today:

Running out of money. We're all living longer. The medical industry has done a great job of keeping us alive longer, with breakthroughs in pharmaceuticals and various treatments. So, we now have an issue that didn't exist 30 or 40 years ago - longevity. A generation ago, people might have died, for example, at age 75. Now, many people are living well into their 90s. And living longer can increase the risk of running out of money.

Healthcare costs. Some people don't want to cut back on their lifestyle in retirement. They wonder, "Can I afford to continue to live the lifestyle I want? Do I have enough money to do that?" This quickly leads to concerns about healthcare costs. As we all know, healthcare costs continue to escalate. Whether you are set up with a great health insurance fund for your retirement or you're self-funding, even people who have a substantial amount of money saved for retirement are concerned about climbing healthcare costs.

The good news is that we know much more about staying healthy – particularly fitness and nutrition – than we used to. That's definitely a positive regarding the healthcare changes that have taken place in the last 20-30 years. Yet we all can't help but think about the costs of staying healthy. Even the retiree who's all set up and has what seems like all the money in the world – which you might think would cause them not to worry at all – is concerned about healthcare costs.

Leaving money for the kids and grandkids. What about helping out your children? Where do you stand when it comes to leaving money to the kids? Do you feel obligated to leave money to kids or grandkids? Or do you feel like you shouldn't leave them anything because you started with nothing? Is there a balance in between? This is another area where it can best be described as different strokes for different folks. It's important, however, that you explore your answer to these questions.

Investment philosophy and strategies. Next, of course, we have to consider your investment philosophy and investment strategies to fund your retirement income. This includes how to navigate disagreements between spouses when it comes to investment philosophy, such as how much risk to take.

And, of course, here in the Northeast where I'm from, there is always a lot of talk about the cost of living. The high taxes and high cost of so many other essentials, leads to frequent conversations about whether or not to relocate to the South, the Southwest, or the Southeast – where clearly not only are taxes lower, but the overall cost of living is lower.

In this book, we are going to be talking about all of these issues, tackling them one at a time, and connecting the dots. So, I want you to sit back, perhaps grab a highlighter, and get started. We're going to go through some strategies and suggestions, and walk through the building blocks for you to maximize your retirement.

1 WHAT'S THE MONEY FOR?

You're thinking about retirement or you're already retired. What's the money for? Why did you sacrifice so long to save that money? Why did you work so hard? Why did you put off purchases or vacations that you could have taken, so you would have an adequate retirement income?

Before you do a projection, before you attempt to figure out how much money you can have coming in every month, before you calculate what rate of return you need on your money, you need to spend a moment or two thinking about what the money is for.

Here's a great way to do that. Take out a piece of paper. In fact, why not do this now. Get a piece of paper, a pen, maybe grab a notebook. Go off in a corner somewhere and just sit and write all the things that you want your ideal retirement to be. What does it look like? Where does it happen? Just sit and dream, and jot down your thoughts.

Pretend that you had no financial constraints whatsoever, that you had all the money you needed. Remove all the obstacles from the equation and just write down the ideal. Go ahead and write it down as you picture what your ideal retirement would look like. If you have a partner, have them in on this, too. As you describe the ideal retirement to each other, write it down.

Let me suggest just a few areas you can start with.

Where do you want to live?

Where's the ideal place to live? Again, forget about financial constraints. Would it be in a big city? Would it be out in the country? Would it be in the northern, southern, eastern, or western United States, or perhaps the southwest? Would it even be in the United States? Where are your kids? Where are your grandkids? (If you have kids and grandkids.) Where are your loved ones? Where do you want to live? That's a great place to start this exercise.

What do you want your activities to be?

Do you want to play golf every day? Do you want to participate in other sporting activities? Do you like to travel? What kind of daily activities will you be doing in retirement? Who will you be with? Great questions! What kind of people – or who specifically – will you be hanging out with? Where do they live? (Yes, we're going back to the "where do you want to live" question.) What type of activities do you enjoy, what sort of people will you be doing those activities with?

Will you have more than one house?

Again, don't think about whether you can afford it or not. If you could, would you like to have more than one house? Or, perhaps you want to live in two places, but you don't want to own a house at all because you hate the yardwork, you hate the maintenance, you hate the unknown of things breaking, and so on. You get the idea. Dream on, and just write, write, write. Get that picture as clear as you possibly can. Be specific. Don't just say "I want to travel," say specifically what destinations you'd like to visit, and how you want to travel. Perhaps you want to travel on a cruise ship. Or maybe you'd like to fly on a private plane. You may prefer to drive. Or your ideal may be to take a cruise from New York City over to Italy and then drive across Europe. Be as specific as possible.

Here are a couple of additional areas you may choose to include:

Who would you like to help?

Many of our clients have significant charitable goals, involvements and activities. So, who would you like to help? Would it be organizations? Would it be individuals? My wife and I just set up college savings plans for our nieces and nephews. Would you like to do something like that? Or perhaps that is not in your plan – giving funds to charity is not something on your list. That is fine, too. No reason you need to feel guilty at all. Your money is your money. They wouldn't call it "giving" if it was an obligation. Giving is giving, of your own free will. That said, is helping other people something you'd like to do?

What about your kids?

Some people don't want to leave any money to their kids or grandkids (if you have grandkids). Others place that high on their list of priorities. It's up to you. This is your list, your dreams, how you'd like to spend the money you've earned and invested. There is no right answer, just your hopes and dreams and goals.

I trust you get the idea. Write completely unconstrained - what are your dreams, what are your goals. If you did not have any kind of money limitations whatsoever, what would your retirement look like? Who would it be with? Where would it happen? How often would you travel? What type of activities would you be involved in?

So, take some time and write those things down now, because in the later chapters of this book, we're going to get into questions such as these: "Are you constrained by anything?" How do you overcome certain obstacles? How do you discuss with a partner any disagreements about what your retirement is going to look like?

It is very important that you start with a blank sheet – the sky's the limit – just dream and write it down. This is the foundation of maximizing your retirement. It's not generic, it's not one size fits all. It is specific to you. And you can't maximize your retirement until you know what the maximum looks like.

WRITE DOWN YOUR DREAMS AND YOUR GOALS.

2 THE BUILDING BLOCKS FOR A SUCCESSFUL RETIREMENT

Many people, when they start to plan their retirement and financial planning for that retirement, begin with their investments. In fact, many financial advisors, if you were to ask for advice on planning for retirement (or even if you are already in retirement) immediately start looking at investments.

From my perspective, this is like deciding to build a house and before you even have a blueprint in hand, focusing on the types of tools you're going to use or the type of lumber you'll use and where it's from. Obviously, the first thing you do when you're building a home is to create a blueprint. That is why you hire an architect, unless you happen to be one. Design the house – that's step one. Make sure that the design is something that can be built from a structural standpoint, and then you begin to hire the people to build the house. Later in the process, you may focus on the tools to get the job done. And maybe, as an owner who is having the house built, you don't even focus on the tools at all, because ultimately the tools aren't what's important. You want the house.

There is a saying that nobody wants a drill, they just want the hole the drill will make. Well, hardly anyone really cares what particular tool somebody uses to build a house, for the most part (unless you're a builder), they just want a good quality house. Planning your retirement is much the same, whether retirement is still ahead for you, or even if you're already retired.

We need to focus, in other words, not on the tools, not on the investments, until later on - after some fundamental questions have been answered. I consider these the foundational building blocks for a successful retirement.

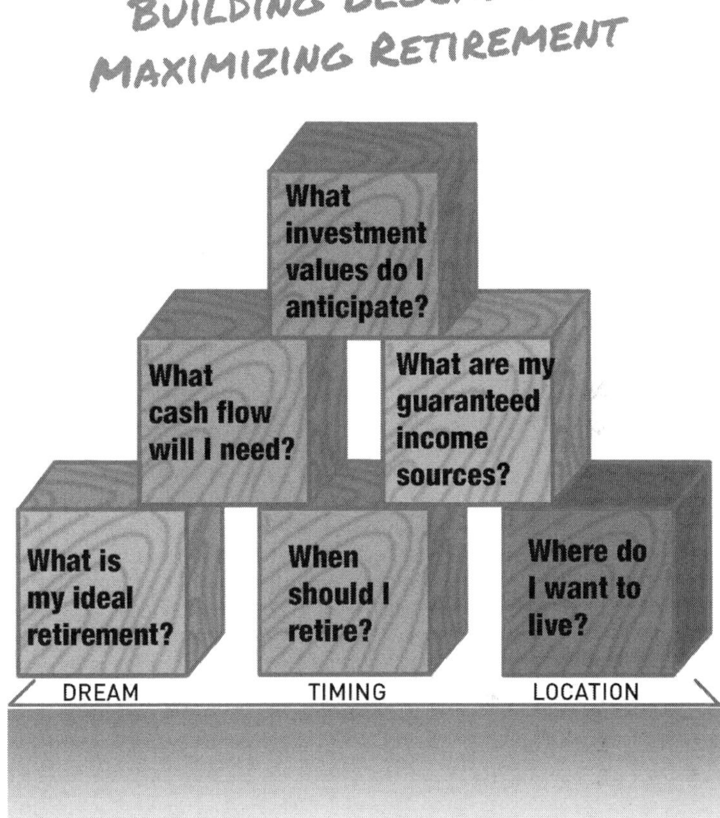

As I explained in Chapter 1, the first building block is to envision the retirement you want. Ask yourself, **what is my ideal retirement**? Dream!

The next building block is **when should I retire?** As we discussed briefly in the previous chapter, timing is everything. If you don't know when you'll want to retire, just pick a date so you can start with a framework.

You could begin by using that date, and you can move it forwards or backwards depending on your financial situation. As before, if you are married or if you have a partner, talk about it with your partner. As you have this conversation, you may discover that at the outset, you may disagree on when to retire. For planning purposes, it's important that you're on the same page.

You may also find that the definition of the word retirement can be very different, depending on who it is. I was talking with somebody recently and they were saying "I don't ever plan to retire." And I responded, "Well, do you plan to not be working in the job that you're working in right now?" To which they answered, "of course, I don't plan to work at this job for all time, but I certainly don't plan to retire."

As the conversation continued, I asked "What does that mean to you?" Turns out that he anticipates doing volunteer work. He might even take on projects from time to time. For example, if he sees that his neighbor needs a project done on his house, he will go over there and help, and so on. In his mind, he is still working; he is not retired. Many of us, I believe, would say that he retired from a job of 25 or 30 years – even if he does an occasional project and some volunteer work. That's why it is important that you define retirement.

When I say to my spouse, I want to retire, – hypothetically; I personally don't want to retire – it means having me just me sit around the house all the time.

Well, I like reading. I like watching movies. I love watching documentaries. But I absolutely would go stir crazy not having anything to do. So my idea of retirement might be taking up a sport or taking up some type of a skill that gets me on the path of starting something all over again. To me, retirement is not sitting around the house.

You see why it's very important that you define retirement, as you consider when you plan to retire. Pick a time. Select a date. And have a discussion with yourself, or with your partner (if you have a partner) – what will that retirement look like?

The next building block is location – **where do I want to live**? As was mentioned earlier, there are multiple elements to this question that deserve some time and attention. What part of the country – or world – would you like to call home? And do you prefer one home, or two, or some other combination. Another aspect that could impact where you want to live is taxes. I'll discuss that in greater detail in the next chapter, as a possible constraint that could affect where you choose to live. All these considerations, taken together, will help you to determine what this building block – where do I want to live – looks like.

Those are the foundational questions – the initial building blocks: Dream (What is my ideal retirement?), Timing (When should I retire?), and Location (Where do I want to live?). Now, we move on to the next building blocks, in which we consider your resources.

Giving thought to **cash flow** is a key building block. What type of cash flow do you want to spend? Immediately, when I say what "do you want to spend," people often respond with "I don't know what inflation is going to be. I don't know what the cost of living is going to be," and so on. Forget about all that. Keep it simple.

A good financial advisor will be able to help you figure out, or will show you historically, what inflation has been - and you can then plug that into a retirement income plan. But what you need to decide is this: if you were retiring today with today's dollars, with the cost of everything that you like to do and all the things that you have to buy today, what would you want coming in that you then could spend?

Let's say you choose $10,000.00 a month. It's a nice round number, $10,000.00 a month. Well, a good financial advisor will be able to plug inflation numbers into software and say if you want $10,000.00 a month today, ten years from now you'll need $15,000.00*, because the cost of the things that you buy may go up by about 50 percent ten years from now, based on inflation.

Obviously this is a number that can be discussed and adjusted by a financial advisor, depending what their outlook is and what your outlook is, regarding inflation.

---

* The $15,000 is just an example. The real inflation could be more or less.

But again, this is in the context of our earlier building blocks, as we project your cash flow objectives. How much income do you want, in today's dollars? Think about your definition of retirement, and also think about what you and your partner are going to want to spend your money on. Is it more travel? Is it less travel? Is it less fuel? You don't have to be super-specific here, but I'll tell you this: my parents spent a lot more money during the first ten years after they were 65, than they're spending now in their 80s. That's because things are different. They can't do as much. Needs change, even in retirement.

As best you can, think through the ideal situation. This is where a lot of people get bogged down when thinking about a retirement income plan, and building a great retirement income. They just don't know. What I say is, get it 80 percent right. It's never going to be perfect. You're always going to have unknowns. You're going to change your mind about the things you would like to do. Your kids are going to move away or they're going to move closer. There are so many things that can – and will – change, so get it to about 80 percent. Just feel comfortable that you're in the ballpark. Give yourself permission to be 80 percent accurate here, and go ahead to figure out what kind of cash flow you need, in today's dollars.

Now that we have a sense of when and where you're going to retire, and what level of cash flow you want, adjusted for inflation, we move on to the next building block - where are your guaranteed income sources? Typically, for most people, it is Social Security. For some people, depending on what their profession was, there may also be a pension. Sometimes there is a pension where you receive a monthly payment, but you may also have an option to roll over that pension into an Individual Retirement Account. That can provide more flexibility and control. More on that later, when discuss pensions.

For right now, we're asking this question: what are your **guaranteed income sources**? Are there guaranteed income sources? This is an essential question because you don't have to drive all your retirement income from your investments if you have guaranteed income sources. For example, if you have a spouse or partner, you might end up with let's say, $5,000.00 a month from Social Security, between the two of you.

If that's the case, and you wanted $10,000.00 a month, guess what? Now you don't need to create $10,000.00 from your investments. You only need to create $5,000.00 from your investments because guaranteed sources of income like Social Security are providing $5,000.00.

That is the next building block. What are your guaranteed income sources? That's what a good financial advisor will factor in when they're figuring out how to build a great retirement plan for you.

Next, we're going to look at **investment values**. Let's say you've figured out your desired income need. You've decided when you're going to retire. You've determined the guaranteed sources of income. Now we make this assessment: If I want to retire ten years from now, and I have X amount of dollars saved in my investments, will I be able to do that ten years from now? Will my investments be able to create the income that makes up for the shortfall between my desired income and my guaranteed sources of income?

To use my earlier example, let's say your desired income in today's dollars is $10,000.00 a month and we know that Social Security and pensions will provide $5,000.00 a month. Well, now you need to have enough from investments to create that other $5,000.00 a month to make sure you won't run out of money before you die. (Or some of you may want to leave money behind. We'll talk about that later in the book.)

So what are those current investment values? Assuming a reasonable rate of return, what will they grow to at that time? Some people do this and find out right away that they don't really need to save any more money. That's with an assumed interest rate and a reasonable assumed rate of return on their investments. Certainly, that's great news, because that means all your needs are taken care of and if you want to continue to save money, it would be for what you want, beyond what you need. With basic needs taken care of, you can consider:

What do you want to do with that money? What kind of flexibility do you want in retirement?

This would be where you can dream once again, or return to that ideal retirement list you wrote down at the very beginning. You certainly don't have to decide everything right now.

Other people will find out they're likely to fall short, and they've got to save a certain amount of money every month to make sure to meet their income goal. With a good financial advisor, you can have a conversation about how much money you need to save, and what rate of return you will need to earn on those investments.

Let's go back to the scenario we talked about, in which the objective is $10,000.00 a month in retirement income. You have $5,000.00 coming in from guaranteed sources, so you need an additional $5,000.00 from your investments. What rate of return do you need to get on your current investments to provide that $5,000.00, looking ahead to sometime in the future? Is it four percent? Is it eight percent? If you only need four percent, you can be very conservative with your investments. Being aggressive may not be necessary. You could be, of course, if you choose to, but you can decide to be very conservative. If it's eight percent, different story. You're going to need to accept some volatility, a little bit of a roller coaster ride in the market from time-to-time, because historically you can't get eight percent in a straight line going forward – certainly not in today's interest rate environment.

And another factor to consider is how much do you need to save every single month? Only after you answer these questions should you begin to focus on the investments.

It is really unfortunate that often in the world of financial planning, people go to a financial advisor and instead of the financial advisor having this deep discussion, it just doesn't happen. And this isn't the case all the time, but it does occur way too often. There really should be a lengthy, detailed discussion about your fears, your goals, your dreams, what you want your income to be, where do you think you'll live? It is a conversation that should precede a discussion about your investments. Some financial advisors by-pass all of these questions that may be more emotional, or more instinctual, in nature. But they're more to the core of who you are, which obviously is critical to a successful and satisfying retirement.

ONLY AFTER YOU ANSWER THESE QUESTIONS SHOULD YOU BEGIN TO FOCUS ON THE INVESTMENTS.

Rather, some investment advisors begin by looking at your investment statements. They want to demonstrate that they can do this better than their competitor up the street. You may recognize these comments: "You shouldn't own this." "This is great, so why don't you own more of this?" "Why haven't you done this?"

In my view, that focus is all wrong. Go back to my analogy of building a home. If you're going to build a home, you don't start by trying to figure out which hammer to use. (Okay. You might have a favorite hammer. That's not the point.) The point is, you've got to design the home. You've got to make sure that home can be built, that your expectations are realistic. You've got to determine, if you have a budget, that it fits within your budget. All kinds of things need to be done *before* you decide whether to use a Makita drill or a Milwaukee drill to drill the holes that you'll need to build the home.

Once again, I return to that analogy of the drill. Nobody wants to buy a drill. They want the hole - and they have to buy the drill to get the hole. If you could just get the hole, you could skip the drill. If you could just wave a magic wand and have the retirement income you need, you would not have to focus on the investments. But for most people, they will need to focus on the investments. But not first. After you've taken the other steps – the other building blocks –is when to begin looking at investments. Not earlier in the process. That's why I refer to them as building blocks.

One builds on another, and together they provide the framework you need.

To review, these are the building blocks for building a good retirement income plan:

1) Dream! - What is my ideal retirement?

Think unencumbered by any limitations. If anything and everything were possible, what would your retirement look like? What would you want to do?

2) Timing - When should I retire?

Do you love your job and want to stay in it as long as possible, or are you someone who can't wait to retire? Or perhaps somewhere in between? Give some thought to the factors we've discussed, and select a day you plan to retire.

3) Location - Where do I want to live?

What are your preferences – where you are, or somewhere else? Consider your dreams and your timing, and the range of possibilities. What would work best for you?

4) What cash flow will I need?

In today's dollars, if you were retired, how much cash flow do you want coming in? Evaluate the various aspects that impact what you'll need, and what you want, to have available to spend every month.

5) What are my guaranteed income sources?

What are those guaranteed sources of income that we know are going to be there? Social Security, pensions, so on. It could also be a trust fund, by the way, among those guaranteed sources of income. So, any kind of guaranteed source of income.

6) What investment values do I anticipate?

What are your current investment values? Then we plug in the numbers and do some math, which leads to projections of future investment values, and whether there is a shortfall.

We will continue to go deeper into each of these items in the coming chapters. You're probably thinking, ok, that will be helpful, but wait a minute, you haven't talked about healthcare and healthcare expenses. You haven't touched on taxes, and the impact taxes have on retirement planning and retirement. And so on. Not to worry. There's more to come on those issues, and some unknown factors – things that are almost impossible to know, but we've got to consider. We began with the six essential building blocks – the foundation for a successful retirement.

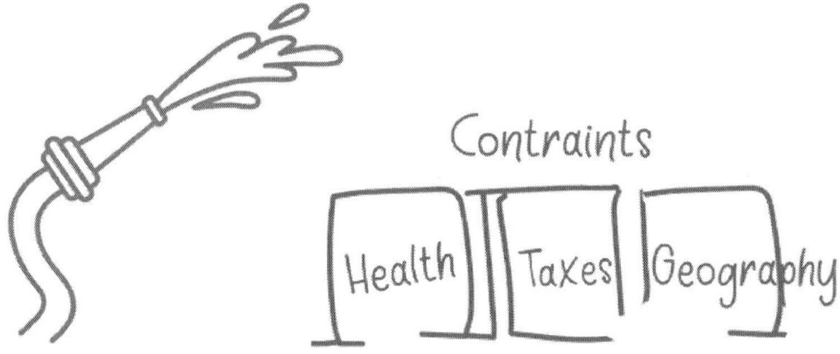

3 CONSIDERING YOUR CONSTRAINTS TO A REWARDING RETIREMENT

Now that we've talked about the building blocks for a successful retirement, it is important that we take a look at the other side of the coin – the constraints or obstacles to achieving the rewarding retirement that you've worked for.

So, let's talk about the constraints that you may encounter, and how to navigate past them. We'll begin by going to that list you made – your dream list that you wrote down, unencumbered by any constraints whatsoever.

Looking at the list, thinking about your dream retirement fantasy, do you have any constraints? Are there any obstacles that could prevent a satisfying retirement?

What would a constraint be? A constraint could be anything. Here's one way to look at it. Picture a garden hose, or a fire hose, and you put a hose clamp on it and start tightening that clamp. You're creating a constraint - the water cannot flow as fast or as easily through that hose. It is very much the same with any type of business or any type of goal that we have – we need to ask the question, what are the constraints? What will slow down, or get in the way of, what we're trying to achieve? Or, you may look at it this way - what will pour cold water on your hopes and dreams for retirement?

Typically, if we can remove or deal with the constraints, then we can achieve a better outcome. In this case, for a great retirement, we have to think ahead about what our constraints would likely be. Sometimes constraints can be removed, other times they cannot. So what would our constraints likely be? And how do we tackle them?

IDENTIFY

THE OBSTACLES THAT COULD PREVENT A SATISFYING RETIREMENT?

Health would probably be the first category that comes to mind. Are you healthy enough to do all the things you want to do? The good news today is that we know more about nutrition and exercise – and health supplements are much higher quality – than ever before. In fact, you can go to doctors that specialize in longevity, responding to illnesses or diseases that afflict people over 65, or over 70, years old. You probably know someone who has rebounded from an illness, or managed to stay healthy, where years ago that might not have been possible. Today, it is.

They're even working on combatting illnesses, including Alzheimer's and Parkinson's, which for many years we thought would not have treatments. And so, the good news is, even if you have a health constraint, there may be a way to deal with it to have a higher quality retirement. So, health could be one constraint.

Another constraint could be geography. If you live in Alaska and you can't afford to travel, it's unlikely you're going to spend a lot of time on the beach. That may be an extreme example, but you get the idea. So, think about all the possible constraints regarding geography that might impact the retirement of your dreams. And you may want to consider ways to adjust your geography – perhaps relocating, or having two houses, or living in multiple locations at different times of the year - if you believe where you are geographically could be an obstacle to realizing your retirement objectives.

Right off the top of my head, I can think of health, and geographical location. Next – and this is no surprise - I also think of money as a possible constraint – which is why I'm writing this book. Of course, when you think of money, you probably also think about taxes – they do tend to go hand-in-hand. So that's definitely a possible constraint – money and taxes. More on that in our upcoming chapters.

Now, think just briefly about what your constraints are, as we move on to discuss the building blocks in greater depth, and delve into how to maximize your retirement.

4 WHEN SHOULD I RETIRE?

When should you retire? That is the question, isn't it?

If I ask my children – ages 21 through 30 – when they think I should retire, they would probably laugh – they're not even thinking about it at all. As we get older, we begin to think about retirement. As a matter of fact, in my experience as a financial planning professional, when I look back at my career and all the people that I've talked with, planning for retirement starts to really kick in around the age when the kids begin graduating from school.

That strain of buying the house, having a family, and so on, and then putting the kids through school, that is all in the rear-view mirror. As that part of our journey concludes, typically, for most of us, in our 40s and 50s, we then start gearing up our thinking towards retirement.

That doesn't mean we don't think of it earlier. My son, who recently started a job at a large corporation, enrolled in his 401(k) and he knows that is his retirement money. I should add that most children – at least my children – don't think Social Security benefits are going to be there for them. They look at it as just an additional tax, and they may be correct, depending on how young they are. But for most of us, we start really feeling the pressure of saving for retirement when we get into our early 50s.

So, as for the question when should you retire, I think the answer becomes clearer the older we get.

Most of the clients that I have worked with, by the time they hit about 55 to 60 years old, have a date in mind. Sometimes it's financially driven, other times they're just tired of working at a job. I can't tell you how many times I've heard somebody say – and this conversation has been taking place for 15 or 20 years now – the company I work for is different than it used to be. It used to be like family. It seemed like people cared. Now it's all about money – they bring the stock price up everywhere. When I go down to the cafeteria, or into an office for a meeting, the stock price is posted on the wall. It just seems like there's an obsession with the stock price, and much less of a human touch.

While that might be the reality, and it probably is, an individual's feelings are also legitimate – and they feel how they feel. But many times it's just that as we get older, we begin to notice things that we didn't notice when we were young and more idealistic. They fall into the ever-growing category of 'things aren't what they used to be.'

So, let's say somebody is in their early 60s and they're asking that pivotal question - when should I retire?

Much of what we're talking about throughout this book will impact that answer. The two biggest influences, I believe, are 1) can I afford to retire, and 2) how much do I hate or love my job? And then, of course, we will need to consider average life expectancy – for how long will you need to draw on that retirement income.

Some people really love their job, and want to work as long as they can. It gives them a sense of meaning, satisfaction and purpose. Other people just can't wait to get out. What we're seeing more and more is that there is a very wide spectrum, with not a whole lot of people in the middle.

One additional observation: there are certain occupations – which will go unnamed – where if you ask somebody at what age do you get a full pension, they'll know to the day when they get that full pension. It's kind of interesting, and it gives you some insight into the mindset, unfortunately, of workers in those industries or governments.

At the beginning of this book, when I asked you to write out your dream retirement, some of you may have immediately thought about when you should retire. If you did, keep that date in your mind. Earlier, we were thinking in the context of having no money limitations at all – but now, as we get closer to retirement, we want to have a date in mind. That's because to do a proper retirement income analysis or projection, we need a date. That's why, for many of our clients, our firm will run multiple dates as part of our analysis and projections.

As an example, let's explore a hypothetical. Let's say I have a friend, a long-time client, who is in the midst of deciding to retire. He is in his early-to-mid 50s. But he saved, he and his wife didn't live beyond their means, paid cash as much as possible, and he socked away as much as he could into a 401(k) and outside savings. So now, he's in the wonderful position of being able to retire. He had a higher-than-average income, and he worked very, very hard. Which means he is able to do some of the things that he wants to do, and is not limited to only the things that he has to do.

TO DO A PROPER RETIREMENT INCOME ANALYSIS OR PROJECTION, **WE NEED A DATE.**

That is somewhat rare in today's world. Most people work well into their 60s. In fact, as of the beginning of 2021, according to the U.S. Census Bureau, the average age of retirement for men is 65 and for women is 63.

As we build a retirement income plan, we have to take into account life expectancy. So if you're 65 today and you're male, you have an average of 18 years of life expectancy. Again, that's just average. The healthier you are, often the more well off you are, the longer you are likely to live. With more money, you are able to pay for extra services such as medical advice or nutrition experts, possibly health retreats, and so on. That is why when we build our retirement income plans, we go out to age 95, beyond the average life expectancy. As a matter of fact, I like to go out even further - I like to project somebody living to age 100. More on that in a later chapter of this book.

This gives you a glimpse of why thinking about when to retire is one of the fundamental building blocks as we're thinking about maximizing our retirement income. In many instances, it is a tradeoff. Either you can retire early and have less income, or you can work somewhat longer and have slightly more income. If you choose to work longer, your quality of life during those last few years of work may not be precisely what you'd prefer, but that decision could work to your advantage in the long run.

5 TAXES IN RETIREMENT

Taxes. We would be remiss if we didn't have a discussion and think through the amount of taxes that you're going to have to pay on your retirement income – and more importantly, explore whether there is a way to minimize those taxes.

Remember, every dollar you pay in taxes is gone – forever. You will not get that dollar back. If, at the end of the year, you're able to get a tax refund, that's just because you overpaid. But if you paid taxes that were required, and the government has that money now, you're not going to see that money again.

So, how do we minimize taxes in retirement?

Well, there are a number of things you can do. First of all, realize where we are right now from a tax standpoint, historically speaking. Here you see a copy of a tax form from a century ago, in 1913. You'll notice that the tax rates are one percent, two percent, three percent, four percent, five percent, and six percent. That's right, not very high.

TO BE FILLED IN BY COLLECTOR.

List No. ....

.... District of ....

Date received ....

Form 1040.

INCOME TAX.

THE PENALTY FOR FAILURE TO HAVE THIS RETURN IN THE HANDS OF THE COLLECTOR OF INTERNAL REVENUE ON OR BEFORE MARCH 1 IS $20 TO $1,000.

(SEE INSTRUCTIONS ON PAGE 4.)

TO BE FILLED IN BY INTERNAL REVENUE BUREAU.

File No. ....

Assessment List ....

Page .... Line ....

UNITED STATES INTERNAL REVENUE.

RETURN OF ANNUAL NET INCOME OF INDIVIDUALS.

(As provided by Act of Congress, approved October 3, 1913.)

RETURN OF NET INCOME RECEIVED OR ACCRUED DURING THE YEAR ENDED DECEMBER 31, 191 ....

(FOR THE YEAR 1913, FROM MARCH 1, TO DECEMBER 31.)

Filed by (or for) .... of ....
(Full name of individual.) (Street and No.)

in the City, Town, or Post Office of .... State of ....
(See pages 2 and 3 before making entries below.)

1. Gross Income (see page 2, line 12)	$
2. General Deductions (see page 3, line 7)	$
3. Net Income	$

Deductions and exemptions allowed in computing income subject to the normal tax of 1 per cent.

4. Dividends and net earnings received or accrued, of corporations, etc., subject to like tax. (See page 2, line 11)	$
5. Amount of income on which the normal tax has been deducted and withheld at the source. (See page 2, line 9, column A)	
6. Specific exemption of $3,000 or $4,000, as the case may be. (See Instructions 3 and 19)	

Total deductions and exemptions. (Items 4, 5, and 6)	$
7. Taxable Income on which the normal tax of 1 per cent is to be calculated. (See Instruction 3) .	$

8. When the net income shown above on line 3 exceeds $20,000, the additional tax thereon must be calculated as per schedule below:

	INCOME.	TAX.
1 per cent on amount over $20,000 and not exceeding $50,000 . .	$	$
2 " " 50,000 " " 75,000 . .		
3 " " 75,000 " " 100,000 . .		
4 " " 100,000 " " 250,000 . .		
5 " " 250,000 " " 500,000 . .		
6 " " 500,000		

Total additional or super tax	$
Total normal tax (1 per cent of amount entered on line 7) . .	$
Total tax liability	$

What are they now? Well, in 2020, after the tax cuts that took place during the Trump administration, the highest federal bracket was 37 percent, plus 3.8 percent for the Affordable Care Act (Obamacare) tax. Right there, we are up to 40.8 percent. If you live in a state in the Northeast, you can probably add another five to eight percent to that. So already you're creeping up to 50 percent in the top bracket on the last dollars you earn.

Let's compare that to what the top rates were in the '50s, '60s, and '70s. During that 30-year period of time, the top rate was actually 70 percent – and that's just the federal tax rate. Imagine if you live in California – and some of you may live in California – the top tax rate in 2020 was 13 or 14 percent on your income. So, whatever your federal tax rate is, if you live in California, for example, you add 13 or 14 percent.

Some of you may recall this story about Phil Mickelson, a few years back. He was going to move out of California because he figured in his bracket, over 60 percent of the money he earned was going to the federal government. Tony Robbins, as many of you may have heard, did move from California to Florida for this very reason. You might say, well, they're wealthy so they shouldn't mind paying taxes. But even for a wealthy person, if they don't have to pay a dollar in taxes, consider what they might do with that dollar. Two options: they can save it, or they can spend it.

If they save it, it will probably go into stocks, bonds, or something that benefits the economy because they're investing in companies, and there are employees that work for those companies. If they spend it, it also benefits the economy, because they're going to spend it on something. If they buy another car, people built that car. If they're going to eat out at restaurants, people work in those restaurants. If they're going to take a cruise, people work on that cruise ship.

Bottom line: rarely is it better to pay more in taxes, and rarely in my opinion, is it better for the federal government to increase taxes. Some of you may think that is a political statement; it is not. I have never seen a case where it's better off for a dollar to go into the federal tax bucket versus somebody keeping it in their pocket and possibly spending it locally.

Of course, I understand that federal tax dollars are necessary for our government to pay its bills. My son is in the military, and he is being paid with tax dollars. But when we have a discussion about needs, I personally believe that somebody paying 25, 30, 35 percent in taxes - that's just about enough. Why should somebody who earns a million dollars a year go out and earn an extra million if they're going to give 50 or 60 percent to the federal government? I realize I'm talking about very high incomes that very few of you have, but the point is, don't pay more in taxes than you have to. Whatever your income level.

And you may say, "Joel, the tax bill is the tax bill, the tax rate is the tax rate." Well, not necessarily - because the goal of good financial planning, good income planning, and good retirement income planning, is to reduce your taxes over your lifetime, not just for today. Here's an example. Let's say the top federal tax rate is 40 percent, and I have money in a 401(k) or a traditional IRA – let's say I have a million dollars. If I leave that money there, and taxes increase in the future, every time I take a dollar out I'm going to pay more than the 40 percent that I would pay today. Again, this is an example.

Look at it this way. Every time a dollar grows in that account, I'm partners with IRS for 40 percent. When my kids inherit that, under the current rules, they have to take all that money out over 10 years and they would have to pay whatever, based on their current tax bracket. And when I die, if I die at life expectancy, they're probably in their peak earning years, in their late 50s. They're going to be earning probably more money than they ever have in their life and I'm going to dump on them an IRA that they have to take out over 10 years. The result? They're going to get whacked really hard with taxes.

What can I do about that? If I think taxes are going to increase, I could do a Roth conversion. A Roth conversion is simply taking money in a qualified traditional retirement plan, where I have to pay taxes on it when

I take the money out, and rolling it over into a Roth account where I pay some taxes now but in the future I don't ever have to pay taxes as long as the money stays in there, and when it comes out, I don't have to pay taxes as I spend that money. There are a few relatively minor rules regarding putting money into a Roth account. For example, there is a five-year rule. We won't get into the details here, because it's not relevant to the discussion we're having now.

The point to remember, as you plan for your retirement, is that you could pay taxes today so you won't have to pay them later. So, for example, let's say I took a million dollars and converted it from a traditional account over to a Roth account. And using a 40 percent tax rate, I'm going to owe $400,000.00 to the federal government. That means I will need to have $400,000.00 to pay in taxes – and I should pay that from another source, other than the money that was converted. If I write a check for $400,000.00 now – that allows the million dollars to remain in this account, which can grow.

How does that make a difference? First of all, if tax rates go up, I'm better off because when I take money out of that Roth account, it's tax free. If I had left it in the traditional account, and then taken it out, tax rates would have been higher than the current 40 percent.

Secondly, if my kids inherit that money, I have, in a sense, reduced my estate by having already paid the tax for them. They will get more money, and if I am fortunate enough, there will be less money in the estate, and thereby less money to be taxed, because I paid that $400,000.00 already. Doing so will have reduced my taxable estate.

That is an illustration of why it is important that you do tax planning for maximizing retirement income. I don't know what your income is, so I can't know the exact tax planning steps that would be recommended in your specific circumstances, but I wanted to share this fundamental concept - paying taxes today so that you will pay less in the future.

Beyond that, there are other ways to pay less in taxes. If you still work, if you're a private contractor, or perhaps you've retired from your main job but you're doing some consulting, you can set up an individual retirement account or a private pension plan where you would receive a tax deduction for putting money into the account.

PAY TAXES TODAY SO THAT YOU WILL **PAY LESS** IN THE FUTURE

There is also a way to impact taxes on your Social Security payments. Maybe you only pay the maximum every other year, because of the way you have created your income cash flow.

Or maybe one year you take income or cash flow in retirement from a source where you don't have to pay income tax, thus reducing your taxable income, which will reduce the taxes on your Social Security. And the other year you take more money out, or you take the income from a different source the year you have to pay taxes on your Social Security. In this scenario, you are paying taxes on your Social Security only every other year, by being smart about the source of your income each year.

I'm sure you now have a sense of how important the subject of taxes is to your retirement planning. There are any number of strategies that can result in you paying less in taxes than you would have otherwise. The likelihood of achieving that goal increases if you begin planning for retirement sooner rather than later.

6 HEALTHCARE EXPENSES

It wouldn't be prudent to talk about maximizing your retirement income unless we spend some time discussing healthcare expenses. One of the leading constraints preventing people from retiring early is the fact that they may have to go out and buy health insurance. If you are not working, you likely won't have access to an employer sponsored plan, which you probably have had for many years while you were working.

When I say retired and not working, as was mentioned earlier in this book, what I mean is that is you have retired from your main job but you may be working at another a job – something that you want to do, which could be as a volunteer, or perhaps part-time, but not work that provides you with access to healthcare benefits. Maybe it's for a charitable organization and they are willing to pay you a small amount, but health insurance is not included. Or perhaps you work a few hours or days a week for Home Depot or Lowe's or an organization like that, because you like to build things and you want to be in those surroundings. So you're really retired, you have good retirement income, you don't need any more retirement income, but you would like access to health insurance.

You need to keep in mind, as you plan ahead, that if you retire and you don't have access to health insurance, Medicare does not kick in until age 65. Therefore, you also cannot get a Medicare supplement policy until age 65. That is why most people need to go out and get health insurance.

IF YOU RETIRE AND YOU DON'T HAVE ACCESS TO HEALTH INSURANCE, MEDICARE **DOES NOT** KICK IN UNTIL AGE 65

The Affordable Care Act, when it was passed during the Obama administration, created a scenario where people cannot be denied health insurance. It is guaranteed issue, meaning they have to give you a health insurance policy without regard to pre-existing conditions. Typically you can buy that through an exchange that is sponsored by your state, or your state has stepped aside and allowed you to buy direct through the federal government portal. The good news is that it's available. There is also additional good news –premiums are based on your income. You might wonder, why is that good news – my income is high, so how does that help me?"

Here's how. When you're in retirement, you don't necessarily have W2 or earned income from an employer; you may have income coming in, however, from Social Security or perhaps a pension you've triggered early, or possibly from some of your after tax investments. The health insurance premium is based on taxable income, not cash flow. That is a distinction that makes a difference. You see, if I have taxable income coming from a stock portfolio or something like that, I have to report that on my tax return. That is going to influence the amount of my premiums when I buy health insurance through the Affordable Care Act exchange. It comes down to this: the lower my taxable income, the lower my premiums will be.

So now you may be saying, "Joel, wait a minute, how can I change that? How can I lower my taxable income?" Think about this. Let's say you have $300,000.00 in the bank, or in an investment account, and it is invested in very low yielding bonds or something similar. How about if instead of taking a distribution, or income off your retirement portfolio, you decide just to spend down that cash. To continue with that example, say you have $300,000.00 in the bank and you spend $10,000.00 a month. That's going to last you 30 months. What's your taxable income on that? Hardly anything. The only portion that is taxable is the interest, and you're hardly earning any interest.

So, when you file your taxes and you make the calculation based on your taxable income to determine your premium when you buy health insurance through the Exchange under the Affordable Care Act, your cost is going to be extremely low. Then, when you turn 65 and you qualify for Medicare, you can buy a Medicare supplement and then you can change the source of your income.

Until then, you may not want to take money out of your retirement accounts because it is not going to affect your premiums any more than the amount of income you have. I know it does affect Medicare insurance premiums slightly, but the bottom line is that you need some type of health insurance to bridge the gap if you retire before age 65. The good news here is you can manipulate how your income comes to you, or how your cash flow comes to you, and therefore, you can impact of the cost of your premiums.

It is worth mentioning here that Fidelity did a study recently, and they estimated that healthcare expenses in retirement, for the average retired couple, is going to be about $295,000.00. That is $295,000.00 in out-of-pocket healthcare costs, on average, for a couple in retirement. Now, two things to note here. One is that it is a Fidelity study, and second, it is an estimate. Yes, Fidelity is a large company and has a lot of data from which they can make a good estimate – so that probably is a pretty decent ballpark estimate. The key takeaway here is that you've got to set aside something for healthcare expenses, *if you are able to do so.*

Why do I say that? Well, some people just can't afford to. Some people reach retirement and they have their Social Security, they may not have a pension, and maybe they have only a modest amount in investments that they want to live on. For people in those circumstances, it doesn't mean you have to be overwhelmed, or upset, or have a lot of anxiety over healthcare costs. If you can't control it, you can't change it, there is no reason to feel bad about it. That is just what your reality happens to be.

If you have an amount of available money that could be used in this way, you may want to create a reserve account that you want to draw down from, as needed, for health insurance costs. That could be helpful. If you don't have that extra money available, then you have to make a decision as to whether you want to set some money aside and live on less income or perhaps you will decide, for lack of a better phrase, to roll the dice, in the hopes that you won't have those high healthcare costs.

At least some of you are now probably thinking, well, that's kind of odd. Would a financial planner really say that? Well, I'm also a very practical person and a big part of financial planning is how you feel – the peace of mind that you have and the enjoyment that you have in life. And one of the things that I realized very early in this profession is that when you overwhelm people, telling them that they need to do something that they financially just cannot do, they don't do anything. Even when there are other things that they could do.

Many times financial planning is a compromise between the ideal, which you may not have the ability to reach, and what you are able to do practically. Or perhaps it is somewhere in between. But Fidelity is certainly not the only expert in the field to point out that healthcare is going to be very expensive in retirement.

There is one additional possibility to consider. If you are still working, you may have access to what's called a Health Savings Account. Some companies offer what they may call a Health Provisional Account for employees. The advantage of this account is that you put money in on a tax-deductible basis and, as long as the money is spent on qualifying healthcare expenses, you do not have to pay tax when the money comes out.

So if your objective is to save money for a reserve fund and you are not already retired, you can look into contributing the maximum to a Health Savings Account. There's really no downside to it – if you don't spend it on healthcare, it just comes out as it would in a regular retirement plan where, if you took the money out before age 59 ½, you'd pay taxes plus a penalty. The upside, however, is you're saving that money in a pre-tax way so that you can spend it on healthcare expenses.

These are some of the factors to consider as you think about healthcare insurance and the costs of healthcare in retirement. While it is very likely that you will incur healthcare costs, there are a number of ways to prepare for those costs, depending on your resources, preferences and priorities. Healthcare costs can be a constraint in your retirement, but hopefully this chapter has illustrated that there are more options than you may have thought.

7 BEGINNING TO BUILD A RETIREMENT INCOME PLAN

Now, let's get down into the nitty-gritty of building a retirement income plan. It's a financial plan that takes into account both the things that you can reasonably expect, and maybe even some things that you may not know to expect, when it comes to building a retirement plan.

The name of this book is, of course, *Guide to Maximizing Retirement: 6 Key Building Blocks to Success.* And once we get a good handle on any kind of constraints on our dream retirement, such as taxes and healthcare expenses, and we have given some thought to the timing of beginning retirement and where you might want to live, then we need to start devoting some time and attention to maximizing an income plan that is specific to your circumstances. Here's how.

First of all, a few chapters ago, we talked about a hypothetical $10,000.00 a month in income. Depending on where you live in the country, what your history is, how much money you've been spending before you retire, or if you are retired how much money you're spending, that might seem like a high or a low amount, but it's just an easy amount, I think, to get our heads around.

I would say in the Northeast our average client is likely going to spend more than that – sometimes much more than that. If you live in rural mid-America, the cost of living is probably 20 or 30 percent less than it is up in the Northeast. So that is something we consider because it might influence your retirement.

If you are getting the idea that many of these aspects are intertwined and interdependent, you're right. Which is why in developing a comprehensive plan, we need to consider each of these building blocks, and how each will impact our plan to maximize your retirement income.

We've gone through the opening question – what is the money for – and the initial building blocks: what does your ideal retirement look like, when is the right time to retire, and where do you want to live. Each has potential constraints, or factors that can pull you off course, as do the next set of essential building blocks – cash flow, guaranteed sources of income, and investment values. That's why it's important to understand what can go right as well as what can go wrong in any strategy. As was outlined in greater detail earlier in this book, there are factors to consider that are individual to your circumstances, and decisions that need to be made depending upon your goals. All of which are consequential as you begin to build a plan for retirement income.

We've dealt with the first part of building a retirement income plan when we looked at cash flow, which is that amount of money that you want coming in to the house every single month. Now, we want you to forget for just a moment about inflation, we want you to forget about investment return. A good financial planner, with a good retirement analysis and projection tool, will be able to plug those numbers in and should also make sure – through a conversation with you – that you have a realistic expectation of what retirement will look like.

As a side note, one of the advantages of working with a financial advisor that specializes in retirees is you are able to tap into the wisdom of many retirees who have retired before you. For instance, at our firm we have over 3,000 households that we've served – individuals who are either getting close to retirement or are well into retirement. We've seen many of them go through those stages – five years to go to retirement, and then they've retired, and now they're five or 10 years into retirement. So, we've seen the things that they have to deal with. Many of them are things that may not even be on your radar screen at all – things you may not be anticipating if you're not retired yet.

Obviously, there will be things that we just don't know, and can't see into the future about, but you can collectively get some insight and wisdom if you're working with a professional who specializes in retirement planning and has worked with many clients who are, or have been, within five years of retirement on one side or the other. And that collective wisdom – what they have seen their clients go through – can be a significant benefit in developing your retirement income plan.

As was mentioned earlier in this book, timing is everything.

According to the U.S. Census Bureau, the average retirement age for men is 65 and for women is 63. The average life expectancy for a 65-year-old male is 18 years, which means, on average, living to age 83. For a woman, life expectancy is 20 years, so it is a couple of years longer, according to data included in the 2020 Annual Report of the Board of Trustees of the Old-Age, Survivors, and Disability Insurance Trust Funds.

When we build our retirement income plans, however, we don't build only for the average. We go out to age 95. In fact, I like to go out even further - I prefer to project somebody living to age 100. We can't predict what your life expectancy will be, but we believe it's better to be surprised on the positive side than on the negative side. What I'm saying is we want to do our best to make sure that you're not going to run out of money, should you live longer than the average. We have to be very conservative in our assumptions.

For example, at age 65 we have the average expectancy for a woman bringing her to age 85, but that shouldn't mean you plan on only getting retirement checks every month until age 85. Because that is only an average, and in our experience most of our clients exceed that average and live longer because they have extra money and have done a good job saving for retirement. They can spend more money on exercise, better food, yoga, travel, etc. People who participate in theses activities tend to be healthier physically and emotionally. We design plans with our clients so the income will continue for many years, well beyond average life expectancy.

The next two of our building blocks – guaranteed sources of income and investment values – continue to move us forward in developing your plan, and advancing our efforts aimed at maximizing your retirement income.

8 GUARANTEED SOURCES OF INCOME

In the previous chapter we started talking about building our retirement income plan and using a specific dollar amount to start the conversation. So let's pick up where we left off, using $10,000.00 a month. But, as the saying goes, not so fast. Everybody knows that if it is costing me $10,000.00 a month to live today, there's something we're all familiar with called inflation, which means the cost of living goes up. The result is that 10 years from now it will cost more than $10,000.00 a month to do all the things I can do today with $10,000.00 a month. And that is a factor which is very important to consider in our planning.

Historical inflation rates have averaged just over two percent annually during the last 20 years. As we know, some years the inflation rate was higher, some years less, but over two decades, inflation has a significant impact. According to the U.S. Bureau of Labor Statistics CPI Calculator, to have the same purchasing power today as $10,000 in 2000, you'd need $15,431. Using that assumption, based on the history of the past two decades, that means that if you retire at age 65, by the time you're 75, you'll need more than $12,000 a month – and by the time you are 85, you'd need more than $15,000 a month – to do the things that $10,000 did for you at age 65.

Remember 1978-1982? Some of you do. Inflation was well over 10%. Why is this important? Well, it's definitely more important than it used to be, because people are simply living longer. We've talked earlier in this book about health and nutrition and medical science and so on, and we know this to be true from what we see among family and friends – people are living longer.

Longevity makes a difference. Fifty years ago, when people generally would have spent five, six, or seven years in retirement, inflation was not much of a factor that we needed to consider. Now it is fundamental to our planning, particularly as we consider healthcare and other costs. We have to make sure we are able to increase the money we have available every year so that we can keep up with inflation.

That is why, when we use our software program to develop retirement income analysis and projections, we often factor in a three percent increase every year.

We want to achieve a three percent raise, every single year. Historically speaking – certainly over the last 20 years – that has been a fairly safe assumption on which to build a retirement income plan.

Some clients prefer to be even more conservative than that. They will say things like, "Well, the federal government is borrowing all this money, they have all this stimulus happening. I might want to consider a four or five percent long-term inflation rate and plan accordingly." That is a fairly high amount to have to build in increases, especially month after month, year after year, over a long period time, but that doesn't mean it couldn't happen. The past is not always a predictor of the future. So obviously, this needs to be customized for you, consistent with your preferences.

The key here is that people are living longer and we need to account for inflation. Today, it is very possible that if you spend 30 years in retirement, you may need to triple your income in retirement just to keep up with the cost of living.

PEOPLE ARE LIVING LONGER AND WE NEED TO ACCOUNT FOR **INFLATION**.

Once we get a real handle on projected needs in retirement, using $10,000.00 a month as an example at the start of retirement, and then giving three percent increases every year, what we do next is take a look at our guaranteed income sources. Most people are eligible for Social Security, which is what I would consider a guaranteed income source, so that's where we look first.

As soon as I say that, you may respond with, "Wait a minute, Social Security is going to go broke - it might not be there for me." I understand that concern, however, I would disagree with that if you are over 60 years old, and certainly if you are 65 or older. I believe that the promises that were made to you by the federal government when it comes to Social Security will hold. I don't think they're going to renege on these promises for people that are over age 55.

Remember, as I write this, I'm 58 years old, and part of a demographic that votes. I vote, you vote. Who doesn't vote? I don't want to disparage any particular age group, but I think we all have a sense of who doesn't vote. And the last thing politicians want to do is have a lot of people who are over 55 years old angry at them, voting the other way, or having AARP publishing articles saying a particular political party, or politician, is not in our court, not keeping a commitment made by the federal government, and so on. That's why I believe we can count on Social Security, certainly if you're 55 or 60 years of age or older. That is an opinion, but I believe in that opinion. My children, on the other hand, probably shouldn't count on Social Security.

So, to begin, we have Social Security as a guaranteed income source. According to AARP, the average Social Security check in 2021 is $1,543.00 a month. That is the average Social Security check for somebody retiring today. And that number, obviously, goes up slightly each year. Somebody retiring at another time, in the future, will receive a somewhat higher monthly benefit, because Social Security is indexed with a cost-of-living formula. And many of you, if you're higher earners, could be receiving about $2,000.00 or $3,000.00 a month, depending upon when you file, whether it is at age 62, or a few years later. The maximum benefit now is just over $3,800.00 a month, for somebody who files for Social Security at age 70. Bottom line: Social Security benefits continue to go up.

But let's just take that average for 2021 of $1,543.00 a month. That means if you're married, and your spouse also receives that average, that's over $3,000.00 a month in Social Security income. So again, using our hypothetical number of $10,000.00 a month, some of that is already covered - it doesn't all have to come from our investments. So, if we have $10,000.00 a month as the objective and we're getting $3,000.00 a month from Social Security, which will have some degree of indexing for inflation, that's good news. Part of our need is already covered, and we only need to make up for the remaining $7,000.00 or so in income per month.

Example of a **Retirement Income Plan Summary** ROR 6%

Year	John Age	Jane Age	Net Monthly Income	Net Monthly Expenses	Net Monthly Cash Flow	Retirement Funds
						$2,250,000
2021	60	60	$0	$10,224	- $10,224	$2,261,136
2022	61	61	$0	$10,531	- $10,531	$2,256,435
2023	62	62	$5,000	$10,847	- $5,847	$2,294,676
2024	63	63	$5,083	$11,172	- $6,089	$2,334,982
2025	64	64	$5,166	$11,507	- $6,341	$2,373,351
2026	65	65	$5,252	$11,853	- $6,601	$2,409,435
2027	66	66	$5,338	$12,208	- $6,870	$2,443,522
2028	67	67	$5,425	$12,574	- $7,149	$2,474,856
2029	68	68	$5,513	$12,952	- $7,439	$2,502,988
2030	69	69	$5,603	$13,340	- $7,737	$2,527,513
2031	70	70	$5,694	$13,740	- $8,046	$2,548,017
2032	71	71	$5,786	$14,153	- $8,367	$2,564,074
2033	72	72	$5,881	$14,577	- $8,696	$2,575,222
2034	73	73	$5,977	$15,015	- $9,038	$2,580,945
2035	74	74	$6,074	$15,465	- $9,391	$2,580,577
2036	75	75	$6,173	$15,929	- $9,756	$2,573,485
2037	76	76	$6,273	$16,407	-$10,134	$2,559,030
2038	77	77	$6,376	$16,899	-$10,523	$2,536,530
2039	78	78	$6,480	$17,406	-$10,926	$2,505,260
2040	79	79	$6,586	$17,928	-$11,342	$2,464,427
2041	80	80	$6,693	$18,466	-$11,773	$2,413,195

Net Monthly Income is income from Social Security.

Net Monthly Expenses are the desired income; we started at $10,000 per month then increased each year for inflation.

Net Monthly Cash Flow is the amount that needs to be withdrawn from investment accounts each month.

Retirement Funds is the balance in the retirement accounts after withdrawals.

This chart is for illustration purposes only. Any individual results will most likely be different. The ROR is purely hypothetical and not a guarantee in any way.

As we talk about the guaranteed sources of income, certainly some of you have pensions. I'm talking about a defined benefit pension plan here, where the company or the organization has said they're going to pay you every month for the rest of your life. That's guaranteed monthly income for your lifetime, in most circumstances.

You also have the choice, when you take that pension (in almost every case), to cover just yourself for your lifetime or to add another person, typically a spouse, to that pension. It might say something like this, for example: If you retire today at age 65, you're going to get $3,000.00 a month for as long as you live. If you want to add your spouse, so that it will be guaranteed that if she or he outlives you, your spouse would continue to get those payments for the rest of their life. But that's not a free option.

If the benefit is $3,000.00 a month, for example, if one individual is covered for life, to cover both lives for the remainder of their life expectancy, the benefit you receive would be reduced – it might be about $2,500.00 a month, instead of $3,000.00. It's similar to buying life insurance actually. You take a reduction in the check that you could get - you give up some of that money – to ensure that your spouse or significant other, if they outlive you, continues to receive those lifetime payments.

By the way, there is also something called pension maximization, or pension max, which is a strategy to maximize a person's pension through the use of life insurance. There's actually a formula, in which you take the amount of disparity between the single life option and the double life option. Using our example, let's say it was going to be $500.00 a month. So if you took an individual lifetime guarantee of $3,000.00 a month versus giving up $500.00 a month to cover a spouse or significant other, so both of would get $2,500.00 a month for as long as you live, that's a $500.00 difference. The question is what if I kept that $500.00, what if I didn't cover my significant other but I took $500.00 a month out my $3,000.00 benefit and bought a life insurance policy? Would the life insurance policy, at $500.00 a month, be sufficient to pay that pension?

Why might that be of interest? Well, let's use me as an example, to illustrate. If I give up $500.00 a month for as long as I live collecting that pension, and if I outlive my wife, then I basically took a $500.00 pay cut for the rest of my life. If I buy insurance with that $500.00 a month, and my spouse passes before me, then I can cancel that insurance and get a raise of $500.00 a month. Or I can keep that insurance and pass that money on to my surviving child tax free.

One last note on guaranteed sources of income. When it comes to a pension, there is a federal guarantee program called the Pension Benefit Guarantee Corporation. If you work for a company and they go bankrupt and don't have the money to pay your pension, the federal government steps in. It is an insurance program similar to FDIC, which you're probably familiar with; FDIC guarantees your bank deposits. The Pension Benefit Guarantee Corporation (PBGC) is a federal program set up to guarantee pensions. As of 2020, for a 65-year-old, the guarantee of that pension is $6,000.00 per month - $6,034.00 per month, to be exact.

So, if I work for a company, let's say it's an airline, because airlines have had a history of bankruptcy. And their guarantee to me, their pension for me, is this: Joel, if you work until age 65, you will receive $6,000.00 a month. But before I can collect on that benefit, they go bankrupt. The federal government would step in and guarantee that pension. In that way, we can feel somewhat secure, if we have a pension from a public company. Important footnotes: The PBGC does not cover a municipal plan if it is in Puerto Rico or Guam. It does not cover those territories. It also does not cover most church plans, and it does not cover some municipals plans. So this is something to take a look at, to determine if it is applicable to your situation, and could be beneficial for you.

One thing regarding pensions that we haven't talked about is the option to do a Lump Sum rollover into an IRA (Individual Retirement Account). Many companies, large and small, want to get out of their long term liability of paying out a monthly pension for life. They offer a lump sum to employees if they will give up the guaranteed income for life. These lump sums can be quite substantial, many times in the hundreds of thousands of dollars. The advantage is that you now have flexibility and control. You can pass the money on to kids and grandkids, you can vary the payments based on your needs, and you can withdraw large sums from time to time for special needs or wants. The tradeoff is that you bear the investment risk.

9 INVESTING IN RETIREMENT: *IT'S ALL ABOUT INCOME*

When investing for retirement, we want to make sure that our income is taken care of first. The principal job of your savings, and all the guaranteed sources of income you have, is to pay you every month so you can do all the things that you want to do, that you've dreamed about doing, for all these years.

That's because there is a fundamental change when you retire. The fundamental change is that all of a sudden you are going from having a paycheck every two weeks, or every month, to not having a paycheck. That is a significant change. Retirement has even been described by some as 30 to 35 years of unemployment. If you retire at age 65, there's a strong possibility that you are going to live to age 90, perhaps even longer, based on current life expectancy tables. So you need to invest for income, and that is a fundamental change from what you've been doing.

When you are 30 or 40 years old, if you are saving and investing for retirement, those dollars that are dedicated for retirement need to be invested from a growth perspective. Those investments are made with as much risk as you can handle, so that when the market goes down – and it will – you don't panic and pull out. You want to go right up to that line, where you can tolerate the volatility of the market, without having it cause you to sell all your investments and sit in cash.

Income First

Then you get to retirement, and that is a comprehensive change in your life. It also should represent a fundamental change in your investment strategy. In my opinion, that shift should really happen about three to five years before retirement. I remember back in 1999 and 2000, there were a lot of retired people, because the market was so high, who did not change their investment philosophy. Then, all of a sudden, in 2000, 2001, 2002, the S&P 500 Index of stocks drops by 47%. And now all of a sudden, because they didn't change their investment strategy, the retirement they envisioned is out the window. In the Bear Market of 2007-2008, the market dropped by 55%. In fact, some people actually had to go back to work to make ends meet, so they could stop pulling money out of their retirement account. All of which underscores why it's all about income. In retirement, it's income first.

Of course, there are some people who have so much money that they don't have to worry about that. If they have $10 million and they have a portfolio that is spinning off three percent in dividends, volatility in the market isn't so much of a concern. They can stay all in stocks, because they can collect that three percent dividend. But most people aren't in that situation. Most people we talk to, if they are savers and they've worked at saving for retirement, might have an average of somewhere between a half a million and $1.5 million saved. Between their Social Security and the money they have saved, if they take a reasonable income stream off of that money, they may have $90,000.00 or $100,000.00 in income. If you have just enough – just barely enough - to enable you to do all the things you want to do, you will probably want to invest with a bias toward protection of principal with a reasonable rate of return.

Pensions

For a moment, think about how a pension invests money and what the job of a pension is. My grandfather had a pension. He worked for a company for many, many years. It was a company named Home Pride, which made jellies and jams and peanut butter and things like that, based in Minneapolis. When he retired, he received a pension. There was money behind that pension, right? There was a pile of money which the company used to pay out that pension, for my grandfather and all their retirees. Now think about the job of that pile of money. What's the main job of that money? To send out a check every month to everybody who had been promised a pension. The job of that money can be summed up this way: Send out that check every month, until they die, so that people never stop receiving that check, which is money they depend on. Well, that's how you should look at your investments in retirement, or at least a portion of them. The checks need to keep on coming.

Do you think a pension manager gets all hung up, because they didn't beat the market with the entire account in a given year? Probably not. Do you think the pension manager is trying to beat the market, at the cost of losing big in some years? Does she say, "Well, I'm gonna beat the market over a long period of time, so I can take lots of risk." No, they're not. That's not how pensions manage money. Pensions try to smooth out the rate of return so that they can deliver the checks. That's what it's all about: deliver checks every month. It comes down to the four words in the title of this chapter: It's all about income. Your planning for retirement is to create the income you want.

Traditionally, pensions have had a pivotal role in retirement planning, and the flow of income during retirement. What came to be known as the "three-legged stool" had pensions, along with Social Security and Investments, as the three foundational pillars upon which your finances in retirement would depend. As anyone who has ever sat on a rickety stool can tell you, if one leg is uneven or unsteady, you could be in for a fall. While it was never envisioned that any one leg of the stool could fully sustain a retirement, having all three stable and robust was always the goal.

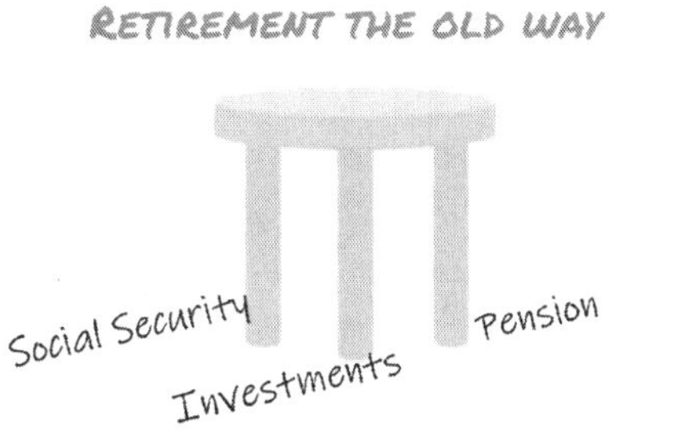

RETIREMENT THE OLD WAY

Social Security
Investments
Pension

RETIREMENT NOW

Social Security
Investments

When pensions go away,
you're left to your own devices.

For pensions, that reliability – a steady flow of checks, month after month – was (and is) essential. Increasingly today, pensions aren't what they used to be, as company financed pensions have given way to a mix of company and employee contributions or defined-contributions plans such as retirement savings accounts. The burden, in many instances, has shifted from the employer to the employee, or some combination. But the objective hasn't changed, from a retirement planning perspective.

Whatever form they take, pensions remain an important segment in funding your retirement. It is, however, important to understand how sturdy that leg is in your own circumstances – because if it is weak, there may need to be a greater reliance on investments to keep your overall retirement plan protected and resilient, and your dream retirement within reach.

Lessons of History

Now, let's talk about some things that have happened historically, and about various investment options.

First, the history. The S&P 500, for the 10 years ending in December 2019, returned about 13.6 percent annualized. So, if you had $1 million in an S&P fund, just a good-old S&P index fund, and you took, let's say 6 percent off of it, which would be $60,000.00 a year, even with all the volatility through those years, you probably did not run out of money. It's more likely than not that you ended the decade with more money than you started with.

By contrast, between 2000 and 2009, the market lost, on average, 0.95 percent per year. So from 2000 to 2009, you lost 0.95 percent per year. There we have one 10-year period where the market returned over 13 percent per year, as measured by the S&P 500, and the previous 10-year period, where there was no gain.

Let's go back to our example. Suppose you retired in 2000. You had $1 million stored up, and you were taking $60,000.00 per year out of your account, and the market didn't grow. In fact, it went down an average of one percent per year. At the end of that ten year period, you've taken $600,000.00 from that account. So you would think you have $400,000.00 remaining, right? Probably not, because, remember, in the years that the market goes down, you have to sell more shares to get your $60,000.00. So it can be a disaster for your retirement income if you're too exposed to either a flat market over a ten-year period, or a substantial amount of volatility. That, in a nutshell, is the challenge we have.

Fear of Missing Out

Your behavior as an investor can also prove to be your biggest challenge to being a successful investor. What do I mean by your behavior? Basically, your emotions - they tend to take over. I know that greed is an ugly word, and nobody likes to admit that they're greedy, so let's look at it this way. Do you ever get concerned, or even scared, that you're missing out? Have you ever had an investment where you thought, "Hey, everybody's making money and I missed out. I should have bought it back on such-and-such a date." An example recently may be Bitcoin. I had somebody ask me, while I was in the midst of writing this book, "Hey, should I buy Bitcoin? It's gone up 500 percent. The guy at the college I go to told me to buy Bitcoin." Well, that's the fear of missing out. Some people would call that greed.

Another aspect of that fear is thinking about the pain of losing money. That's why most people, even people we would consider to be smart, such as engineers and actuaries - individuals who are extremely analytical, and understand that over the long term the market has gone up - even they can panic and sell at the worst possible time. Sometimes their greatest weakness is being so smart. They underestimate the power of their emotions. We need to guard against the fear of missing out, particularly when we know better. Again, we want to invest for income. We want to smooth out our returns.

Stock Market

Just a few paragraphs ago, I mentioned two ten-year periods, the period from 2010-2019, which was preceded by the ten-year period from 2000-2009. We had one decade where the market was basically flat, one decade where the market averaged 13.6 percent. I'll talk more about averages in a moment, because you have to be very careful relying on averages when you're taking money out of a portfolio. But over that 20-year period, the market averaged just a bit better than 6 percent. But when we look at the income we can pull off a stock-market portfolio, we need to be very careful because, as I mentioned earlier, when the market goes down, we have to sell more of what we own to generate the income that we're taking every single year.

Quiz

If you lose 30% in Year 1 and gain 30% in Year 2, what is your average return?

Most people would say zero. But.....

$100,000
30%
$70,000
+ 30%
$91,000

How can you average zero and lose 9%?

Be careful of averages, especially when you're drawing income.

Let me be clear on this. You put in $1 million. You withdrew 6% and you made 6%. You're still at $1 million. What if the market drops, and now it goes down to $750,000.00, and you want your $60,000.00 of income. You're not taking out six percent of your investment like you were when your account was worth $1 million. You're taking out $60,000.00 off of a $750,000.00 portfolio, or eight percent. Now you've lost the opportunity for that money to recover, because you've taken it out of the market. So you see how market volatility works against you. A $750,000 portfolio has to make a 33% return to get back to $1,000,000. Think about that. If you lose 25% in a year, you have to make 33% the following year just to get back to even.

Where else could you put your money? If you don't want to have your money exposed to the stock market, if you want to smooth out rates of return, what options are there, other than stocks? Well, there are a number of options to consider.

Bonds

We could put the money into bonds. If we put the money into bonds, history suggests that we would get a lower rate of return than in stocks, but it should be a smoother rate of return. There will likely be less volatility. It probably will be less of a rollercoaster ride. The challenge here, however, is that we don't have as much of a chance to keep up with inflation with a bond portfolio. But we also have less temptation to sell at the wrong time, which is why a very traditional model for a financial adviser to use when investing for clients is 60 percent stocks and 40 percent bonds. You smooth out the returns of the market, and the hope is that you're going to average somewhere around five to six, maybe five to seven percent. Bonds are there to protect you against the downside. So, that would be one option. Again, we're trying to create retirement income, not a rollercoaster ride of ups and downs and all the emotions that come with it. Remember, again, your retirement should be a time to enjoy. It should not be a time spent worried about your money.

Real Estate

We could invest in real estate, possibly through buying real estate directly. That could be single-family homes, or three- or four-family homes. It might be an apartment building with, say, 12, 25, 100 units. People who have a lot of money can invest in real estate and own it directly. Those with less money, if they want to invest in real estate, need to go into that investment with other people. But the advantage of real estate is that it is a different type of investment - different than stocks or bonds. For example, if you have a building or an apartment complex, people pay rent, usually monthly. So, now you have cash flow. Plus, you have an asset that you own. In addition, there are some tax advantages that accompany investing in real estate. Real estate could allow you, through depreciation, to shelter some cashflow from taxes even while the asset is appreciating in value.

Most people, and most of our clients, don't own real estate directly (and some of those who do, wish they didn't). But you could invest in a real estate mutual fund, or in individual real estate investment trusts. One of them, as an example, is Simon Property Trust. Simon Property Trust owns high-end malls all across the U.S. As an investor, you don't own those malls; you own a sliver of a company that owns those malls. But you will receive many of the beneficial characteristics of a real estate investment. This is just an example of how real estate trust works. Obviously you must be very careful because you could lose money just like in any other investment.

IF YOU OWN A BUILDING WHERE PEOPLE PAY RENT, USUALLY MONTHLY. YOU WILL HAVE **CASH FLOW.**

Again, the idea here is this: How do we blend together a varied portfolio so that you can count on checks coming in every month and have a high probability of not running out of money - perhaps even a guarantee of not out-living your money - to the extent possible.

Guaranteed Insurance Contracts

I'm not going to name every conceivable type of investment on these pages, but another investment that I do want to highlight is guaranteed insurance contracts. You can use guaranteed insurance contracts that are issued by insurance companies and which guarantee your principal. That principal is guaranteed by the full faith and credit of the insurance company, so you want to make certain that you're dealing with a highly-rated, highly reputable company, and you have a specific interest rate that's guaranteed. (These can also be fixed annuities when purchased in smaller amounts.)

Annuities

Another possible investment, which people often include, are annuities. There are four types of annuities, so let's take a moment and briefly discuss each of them. Using me as an example, I own an annuity. My father owns several annuities. In the right circumstances, they make sense. Used poorly, they will disappoint. If you are going to consider annuities, you should know the fundamental differences in the four types of annuities. You also need to be careful if you already own one. You could get in front of a financial advisor who doesn't have a clue on how annuities really work, but will criticize them just to get your business.

Fixed Annuity: The fixed annuity is what I have just described in the paragraph on guaranteed insurance products. You put your money in for, say, five years. They guarantee a certain interest rate, and your principal. The guarantee is backed by the insurance company. There are no fees. At the end of that five-year period, for example, you get all your money back, and you have collected interest along the way. The interest is tax deferred until you take it out.

Variable Annuity: These are the annuities that you hear about most often. You hear a lot of negative comments about them, because the fees are extremely high with a variable annuity, and you're still exposed to the ups and downs of the stock market. You could get a guarantee of minimum income for life, which is very attractive with a variable annuity, but you're paying for that guarantee. So, all in all, we tend not to recommend variable annuities in our company, largely because the fees are so very high.

Immediate Annuity: You could also buy what's called an immediate annuity. This is very much like buying a pension. You take a chunk of money, and you give it to the insurance company. That chunk of money is gone, but what you have purchased looks exactly like a pension. You're going to get a specific amount of dollars every month for as long as you live. For instance, let's say I give $300,000.00 to an insurance company. Maybe they give me a contract that says they are going to pay me $1,500.00 per month for the rest of my life. So I put in the $300,000.00. I'm going to get $18,000.00 a year back, guaranteed, for as long as I live. If I don't live very long, then they keep the money. But if I live for a really long time, I will have received back much more than I put into the insurance company plus I had the guarantee of income for life from the insurance company. What you're really buying, which is why it is important to consider, is the guarantee that you cannot outlive your money. By the way, if you're getting a pension, pay attention to where the deposit is coming from. Many times, it's a big insurance company. If annuities are so terrible, why do some of the biggest companies in the world use annuities to guarantee pension payouts?

Index Annuity: The fourth type of annuity we'll highlight is an index annuity, where you have the potential to earn more interest than the traditional fixed annuity, but you don't have downside risk. The way an index annuity works is first, you put your money in. The principal is guaranteed. Your interest is paid based on the performance of an index.

Here's an example. The annuity calculates the interest they pay based on the S&P 500 index, which consists of blue-chip stocks in the U.S. There are a lot of different parameters here, specific to a given insurance company, so I'm keeping this simple. You could get 50 percent of what the S&P 500 index does in the good years and 0 percent of the downside in the bad years. So let's say you put in half a million dollars, and the market goes up ten percent in that given year. You are probably not going to get ten percent interest, but you might get half of that. So, now you've gone up five percent. The following year, let's say the market drops 20 percent. You don't lose any money. You get to keep the five percent you already made. You never go backwards. The year after that, the market goes up ten percent. You don't have to make up for that loss, so you might make another five percent. Again, you're giving up some of the upside, but you don't absorb any of the downside. That can add up to a lot of peace of mind throughout your retirement. As with any strategy or product, there are pros and cons - so make sure if you are getting outside advice and that you are working with a trustworthy professional. Make sure they are a fiduciary.

Here's the framework we've outlined: You need to identify your income need first. We talked about that in a previous chapter. You need to set up a portfolio, or have the advice of a financial planner to set up a portfolio, that gives you the highest potential rate of return without exposing you to so much risk that you're tempted to do the wrong thing at the wrong time. As was mentioned, often your biggest risk in retirement is your own behavior. So, you ask, "How can I avoid bad behavior?" Answer: You put guardrails around your emotions by creating a portfolio that's not going to go down when times get tough, which will help you to avoid thinking things like, "Oh, I'm missing out. I better go out and buy that stock!"

Create your income plan. Build a balanced portfolio. Monitor it, from time to time. Make adjustments. My suggestion would be that at least some of your money should be safe - in investments that cannot go down, that have some kind of guarantee, whether it's a guarantee from an insurance company, a bank or the U.S. government.

In my opinion, nothing beats the peace of mind that is created by having some safe money. In the good years, you can sell stocks or mutual funds that have gone up when the market goes up, to create your income. In the bad years, you can leave those alone to recover, and you can take some money and some income off of your guaranteed sources. As I said when we began this chapter, the bottom line is that it's all about income. It is. All about income.

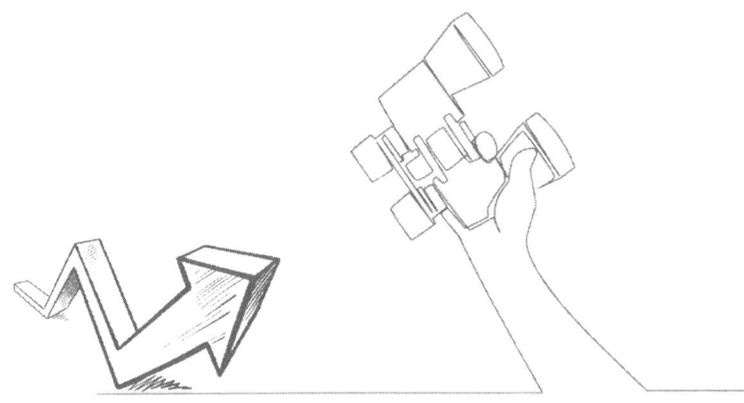

CONCLUSION

In this short book, we've talked about ways to help you get the most out of your retirement by creating the income that will allow you to do many of the things that you've dreamed about doing.

Keep in mind what the goal is here – to live a life without worrying about money. For some of you that will be easier than for others, because some of you have been worried about money for so long that you don't know how to decouple from that worry. To folks in that category I would say, try it – you'll like it! Worry less, enjoy more.

To achieve that goal – retirement without worry about money – it is very, very important that you not only have a retirement income projection, but a plan, tailored for you, your hopes, desires and dreams for retirement. That is probably the most important thing you can do, because you need to know if your money will last as long as you live, based on the amount of income you want and what rate of return you need on your investments, to make that money last.

That is really the key. The other things that I've mentioned – the other building blocks, like where to live, when to retire, accounting for taxes and healthcare expenses and so on – are additional areas that merit consideration. But the bottom line is, what do you need and want to spend, what are your guaranteed sources of income, what do your investments have to throw off to supplement any shortfall, and how do we protect against inflation?

I hope this book has been a benefit to you, and has provided a starting point or a framework for you to think about the elements of effective retirement planning. Please make sure that you get a second opinion from somebody you can trust.

I suggest that you connect with a financial advisor who is a fiduciary. In my view, it is quite important that whoever you deal with is a fiduciary, because they are legally obligated to work in your best interest. I also recommend that person be a Certified Financial Planner (CFP), or that they work at a firm where a member of their team is a CFP. They are also required to act in a fiduciary capacity and they have continuing education requirements, just as most professionals, where they have to stay up-to-date on new or revised rules and laws. This also provides you with an individual committed to a higher level of ethical requirements.

My best wishes to you in your retirement, whether you're already retired, in the midst of planning for retirement, or retirement planning is approaching on the horizon. I consider it a privilege to be in a business where I have the opportunity to help people, as they contemplate and then begin their retirement, to see themselves through their retirement years.

ABOUT THE AUTHOR

JOEL JOHNSON is a Certified Financial Planner™ Professional,® who has been in the financial services industry for over 30 years. He is the Managing Partner at his firm Johnson Brunetti which specializes in working with retirees and pre-retirees in developing in investment, income and estate plans for estates of all sizes. They have helped thousands of families reduce unnecessary income taxes, Social Security taxes and estate taxes.

Joel is author of numerous books on retirement planning, including "The Money Map," and has also been published in Forbes, The Wall Street Journal, Hartford Business Journal and CNBC.com. He hosts a financial segment called "Better Money" on WCVB Boston and WFSB Eyewitness News Hartford as well as the weekly financial radio program, "Money Wisdom." *

* The weekly financial shows for radio and the financial segments on television are paid sponsorships.

WA

Made in the USA
Middletown, DE
01 July 2021